The Little Book About Scholarships

Nancy L. Paul

The Little Book About Scholarships
Copyright © 2014 by Nancy L. Paul

www.TheLittleBookAboutScholarships.com
www.ThreeWishesScholarships.com

ISBN 978-0-9906510-1-7

Photo Credit Jennings Paige Photography.

Getting into college is one thing. Paying for it is another.®

Dedication

To Rebecca, Ari, and Kayla

4

Getting into college is one thing. Paying for it is another.®

Table of Contents

Getting into college is one thing. Paying for it is another.®

Getting into college is one thing. Paying for it is another.®

Acknowledgements

A heartfelt thank you to my three wishes – Rebecca, Ari, and Kayla – for being my guinea pigs and trusting me to guide your pursuit of merit scholarships. We all learned by trial and error when there was no one to guide us through the maze of merit aid.

I am so proud of each of you for your bold efforts to capitalize on your strengths and collectively win $600,000 in merit scholarships. You each have your success stories and it's a pleasure to watch how being rewarded for your diverse achievements has had a positive impact on you.

Thank you, too, to all the panicked parents who shared so openly with me your overwhelm, confusion and frustration with figuring out how to pay less to make your students' college dreams come true; and thank you to all the college-bound students who worked so hard to get admitted and to pursue merit aid.

I also give thanks to the private college counselors with whom I continue to collaborate; the high school counselors who in increasing numbers recognize the need to provide more information and guidance to families who appreciate the many benefits of merit scholarships; the financial advisers and so many other professionals with whom I enjoy a team approach to helping families be wise about money; and even the "nay-sayers" who didn't believe

Getting into college is one thing. Paying for it is another.®

that families needed or wanted help with merit scholarships and who inspire me every day to prove them wrong.

Together, you were the inspiration for *The Little Book About Scholarships*.

Preface

The word I most often hear parents and students use to describe the scholarship process is "overwhelming." It doesn't have to be.

I help college-bound families move from overwhelm to action in pursuit of merit scholarships to lower the cost of college.

Most of us worry and feel guilty that we should have thought more seriously and a lot sooner about paying for college. College deadlines are rapidly approaching and there are big decisions to be made. We know that others are pursuing merit scholarships and we want our students to win "free" money for college, too.

Although scholarships don't have to be paid back, they do require time, effort, and strategy. No one owes students money to reach their college goals. The student – hopefully with parent assistance – must actually do something to deserve and win that "free" money. That includes learning how to find, use, and apply for the right scholarships, as well as achieving in areas that scholarship providers want to reward.

Meanwhile, need-based scholarships require families to complete the government's forms (FAFSA) and follow procedures before being given any financial aid.

Getting into college is one thing. Paying for it is another.®

Unfortunately, private and public high schools nationwide are failing to sufficiently educate families about merit scholarships. Families are left to try to understand the complicated scholarship process for themselves, often haphazardly applying for random scholarships with no real plan. They are wasting valuable time and energy.

Most importantly, families are missing opportunities for college money that doesn't have to be paid back.

I've seen families repeatedly make "less than wise" choices about paying for college, because they don't understand how to leverage their student's achievements to lower the cost of college.

Many families don't plan ahead and they find themselves scrambling to figure out how to pay for college when there are few options left.

Merit scholarships are a great way for families in all financial situations to lower college costs. In addition to the money, there are other benefits to our children pursing merit scholarships.

Even if you can easily pay for your student's first choice college, why would you want to?

There is so much educating to be done around the topic of merit scholarships so that more of our children can be empowered by contributing to the c education, and more families can make inform about how to include merit scholarships in a g reduce college costs.

The most frequently asked questions about scholarships have become predictable for me. They are the same questions I invariably pondered before spending hundreds of hours studying the merit scholarship process for my family and then for my clients.

I have distilled all this information into the topics covered here in this little book. These questions and answers are the most critical to creating your own game plan on the road to money for college! I take out the confusion and give you easy to use guidance – after all, this is *The Little Book About Scholarships*. I want you to read this resource and use it!

I would love to answer any questions that you may have, either in a personal email and/or as the subject of a future article in my newsletter, "The Scholarship Sleuth."

Email your questions to info@ThreeWishesScholarships.com.

Please invite others who can benefit from understanding merit scholarships to join our community. Sign-up at www.ThreeWishesScholarships.com.

Getting into college is one thing. Paying for it is another.®

Here's to your scholarship success!

Nancy.

Getting into college is one thing. Paying for it is another.®

Reality has set in...

Getting into college is one thing.

Paying for it is another. ®

Getting into college is one thing. Paying for it is another.®

Getting into college is one thing. Paying for it is another.®

Introduction

There is no shortage of resources dedicated to giving families advice about paying less for college. Volumes of statistics and information exist analyzing federal aid, loans, cost comparisons of schools, and work/study programs, as well as need-based and merit scholarships.

Huge databases boast 1.5 million private merit scholarships and three-inch thick books promise "billions of dollars in free money for college." Even YouTube videos inform viewers about scholarships and related topics.

However, families are still overwhelmed. They crave a basic understanding of how they can use scholarships to lower the cost of college for their own families. Some don't even realize that merit scholarships - money for college awarded for achievement rather than demonstrated financial need - are an option. They mistakenly believe that scholarships are only available to families who meet strict requirements for need-based aid.

Families are often so confused that they don't even know which questions to ask to help them understand scholarships. They simply don't know what they don't know!

Getting into college is one thing. Paying for it is another.®

Some questions, however, have become standard for me. To address this, most of the content of this book is delivered in two ways: frequently asked questions (FAQs) and questions families SHOULD be asking.

Merit-based scholarships are open to those who qualify for need-based aid; however, the reverse isn't necessarily true. Many students qualify for merit scholarships, even if they do not qualify for need-based aid.

My particular area of expertise is in merit scholarships, as our family continues to leverage our daughters' achievements to reduce the cost of college. Because of my extensive knowledge and research, families nationwide retain my services to help them aggressively pursue merit aid.

Not long ago, I, too, had many sleepless nights pouring over scholarship books and websites seeking answers about how merit scholarships worked, what we needed to do, and how we could benefit from pursuing them.

It was trial by error as I hit one dead-end after another, looking for merit scholarships that fit my oldest daughter, Rebecca. Naively, I presumed that being a strong student in Honors English meant that she would know what to include in a winning scholarship essay.

This little book was born from spending hundreds of hours researching merit scholarships for my children and my clients, and studying the scholarship process in general. You're receiving the benefit of the mistakes and lessons my family learned the hard way!

Looking back, I'm amazed at the amount of wrong information I started with. I was angry and dismayed that our high school guidance counselor and private college counselor didn't feed us key information more readily. It seemed they could have made it so much easier for all of us who were so hungry to learn about merit aid.

More recently, however, I realized that some high school counselors are just too busy to study the complexities of merit aid. Many believe they are already providing enough information to guide their families. Some high school counselors have told me that they don't think their families want or need information about merit scholarships. They're wrong!

Our family had some money set aside, but we still felt stressed about figuring out the smartest way to pay for college. Loans were not an attractive option; invading investment accounts was not an ideal solution either.

After all, we knew other families were being awarded merit scholarships and we wanted the same advantage. Not knowing where else to turn, I invested the time and frustration into my own self-study program! Over 100 hours later, my daughter, Rebecca had a neatly-typed

Getting into college is one thing. Paying for it is another.®

report containing $150,000 of hand-picked merit scholarships she was eligible to receive.

The Little Book About Scholarships is designed to give families a crash course in the basics about merit scholarships. My goal is to simplify the complicated process so that you can move from a state of overwhelm to action in pursuit of money for college that doesn't have to be paid back!

My intent isn't to be vague. Instead, I want to be accurate. Therefore, there are several aspects about scholarships that really do require a personal conversation with a financial aid officer at a particular college. Schools vary dramatically in how they award and handle merit scholarships.

I sincerely hope that the information contained here will propel you to create a game plan to strategically leverage your student's many achievements to win money for college.

It's my pleasure to share with you what I've learned the hard way.

Let's get started!

The Good News First

Chances are that if you're reading this book, you're overwhelmed with figuring out how to be smart about paying for college. You're likely wondering whether or not scholarships can actually help lower the cost of making your student's college dreams come true.

The good news is that virtually anyone can qualify for merit scholarships. Yes, that's right, anyone. Surprised? Your student does not have to be a top scholar or all-star athlete to be rewarded for their achievements.

Not every student, however, will take the necessary steps to leverage their achievements to win money for college. That means doing the right things at the right time.

Many families mistakenly wait to tackle scholarships until after college applications have been submitted. In fact, each year I receive calls from parents hoping to secure scholarships to help pay for a college that their student has already committed to.

That's not how it works.

Start now.

Finding, applying for, and winning merit scholarships takes time, effort and strategy. Certainly, some students will be eligible to receive more merit aid than other students. Be advised that those who engage in well-chosen activities starting in 9th grade are at an advantage.

It's never too soon to be thinking ahead to college and scholarships!

The first step is understanding how merit aid works and how you can use it to lower the cost of college for your family. I wrote this book as your solution to understanding what merit scholarships are, what they aren't, and how you can position your family to receive money for college that doesn't have to be paid back!

Ready for some more good news?

Merit scholarships are available to students in all financial brackets.

Even students from the wealthiest families can win merit scholarships. These prizes are awarded for achievement in an endless number of categories, including academics, community service, ethnicity, athletics, career goals, hobbies, religious beliefs, and more.

I began studying merit scholarships in 2010 when the eldest of my three daughters, Rebecca, was applying to colleges.

We had hired an independent private college counselor, but we could not find anyone to help us understand how merit scholarships could work for our family.

Like so many other families, we didn't qualify for need-based aid. Our daughters are close in age so we were looking for financial assistance to pay for three college educations in three years!

Ultimately, I spent over 100 hours researching merit scholarships before finding $150,000 in private merit scholarships that Rebecca was eligible to receive.

She didn't apply for or win all of them, but the money that she did win made an impact on our family's budget and brought many other benefits that we didn't anticipate.

Non-financial benefits of students being rewarded for their achievements may be more valuable in the long run than the money.

More on that later!

In addition to winning private merit scholarships, Rebecca was offered a total of $300,000 in institutional merit aid. Kayla, my youngest daughter, has been offered over $152,000 in institutional merit aid, and Ari, my middle daughter, has received over $80,000 from two universities alone.

Merit scholarships, especially the private ones, don't just happen. Families need to do the right things soon enough to be successful with securing money for college.

Three Wishes Scholarships – named in honor of my three daughters – is dedicated to saving family's time, reducing stress, and maximizing potential to win money for college. In addition, our company has evolved in scope and services. Our clients are reporting additional benefits of following our signature WISHES Blueprint for College Dollars, a step-by-step system for reducing the cost of college.

The educational landscape is continually changing, especially as it pertains to college. I am constantly studying merit scholarships and other ways to lower college costs.

I invite you to join our community and receive complimentary articles and valuable information at www.ThreeWishesScholarships.com.

Stay up-to-date with the latest scholarship news so that you can sleep better at night, knowing that you are doing your very best to give your student the competitive edge in college and in life.

Frequently Asked Questions

**These are the question I am asked over and over.
They are great questions and you need the answers.**

1. What exactly is a merit scholarship?

A merit scholarship is money for college that is given for achievement, rather than demonstrated financial need. Unlike loans, scholarships do not have to be paid back. This is true of merit-based and need-based scholarships.

Scholarships are an important element for reducing college costs. Some scholarships have both a merit component and a requirement of demonstrated financial need. I call these "hybrid scholarships."

There are two main categories of merit scholarships: private and institutional. Ideally, families will pursue both types, because there are advantages to each. Colleges use institutional merit scholarships to entice top students to attend their school instead of going somewhere else.

Meanwhile, private merit scholarships can be offered by organizations, individuals, or businesses to support the goals of students whose achievements match the mission of that scholarship. Helping a student reach their potential brings the organization closer to reaching its own goals. It's a win-win situation!

Achievements can be anything from academic excellence, community service or leadership, to heritage, career goals, or hobbies, and everything in between. And athletic scholarships are a world all their own!

2.   What's the difference between institutional and private merit scholarships?

It's important that families understand how to use and pursue both private and institutional merit aid to more dramatically lower the cost of college. Standardized test scores and GPA usually count more heavily for institutional merit scholarships than for private scholarships. Meanwhile, private merit aid rewards students for an endless array of achievements.

The main benefit of institutional merit scholarships (and this is a big one) is that they typically offer significantly more money than private merit scholarships.

Institutional awards are generally renewable for four years, which adds to their value in many ways, including their relative predictability and total prize money. This can help tremendously when the family is comparing college costs to determine which schools the family can most easily afford.

Beware, however. Institutional merit scholarships are rarely guaranteed from one year to the next. In order to keep the scholarship, recipients are often required to take a minimum number of units each term and maintain a minimum GPA.

Every school has its own standards. It is critical that a family understands all of the requirements for maintaining a renewable scholarship, especially if they are counting on that scholarship to be able to afford a particular school.

As a group, the most prestigious, high-ranking institutions offer less merit aid because they believe that their status and programs will be enough of a draw for admitted students to choose their school over all others.

Furthermore, some of the highest ranked colleges do not offer any merit scholarships, but are particularly generous with need-based aid.

Middle-tier schools tend to offer the most merit help. They do so in hopes of improving their rankings in *U.S. News and World Report*, for instance, by attracting students with higher standardized test scores, GPAs, and other talents.

Each school has its own standards of selection and requirements, including how much total aid a student may receive from all sources.

Getting into college is one thing. Paying for it is another.®

Be sure to check with the financial aid office at each school your student is considering to fully understand their policies, as well as their opportunities for financial assistance.

Some colleges automatically consider every admitted student for merit aid, while others require a separate application. To make the process even more confusing, there may be different policies for different merit scholarships at the same college.

Individual departments within a college, alumni groups, and college-wide scholarships may all exist at a single school, each with its own eligibility guidelines, methods of selecting winners, restrictions, and purposes.

The disadvantage of institutional merit aid is that the money can only be used at that one college.

I strongly encourage families to include both private and institutional merit scholarships in their game plan to reduce the cost of college.

Private merit scholarships work very differently than institutional aid. Unlike scholarships from colleges, private merit scholarships almost always require that a student apply in order to be considered for the award.

Private merit scholarships offer flexibility and have the benefit of not being tied to one particular college. For this reason, private merit aid is a valuable component of a strategy to reduce college costs.

Most students do not officially commit to attend a particular college until spring of their senior year of high school. In fact, is not uncommon for a student to change their mind at the last minute about where they will go to college. Therefore, pursuing money for college that can be used at multiple schools is a wise investment of time and energy.

The prize amounts for private merit scholarships are typically smaller than institutional merit aid and they are often not renewable. Top awards can range from a few hundred dollars for local scholarships to tens of thousands for national competitions.

Some merit scholarships have restrictions concerning how the money can be used. For instance, some awards state that the scholarship can only be used for tuition, while others allow the funds to go toward tuition, books, and other college expenses.

A private scholarship may also specify a particular geographical region, or require that the funds only be used at a four-year college, rather than at a community college or technical school. Every private merit scholarship has its own standards, rules, application, etc.

According to www.fastweb.com, a scholarship website, there are 1.5 million private merit scholarships. This means that there are 1.5 million opportunities to find private merit aid that fits your student! That's a blessing...and a curse! Digging for private scholarships that your student is eligible to receive can be a daunting task and very time-consuming.

On the positive side, there are virtually endless opportunities for private merit aid. New private scholarships are continually emerging throughout the year.

Comparatively speaking, private merit scholarships tend to place the most value on non-academic achievements. Private scholarships revolving around academics do exist; however, students competing for private scholarships have many more ways to showcase their achievements beyond their test scores and GPA.

Private scholarship judges strive to reward candidates whose character, goals, and involvements reflect the group's mission. Community service, artistic talent, and being the first in one's family to go to college, are among the many diverse qualities that private scholarship judges want to support with money for college. These judges are looking for candidates whose achievements are viewed to indicate potential for future success in areas important to the scholarship's mission.

Here's a brief summary of the highlights of most institutional and private merit scholarships:

Institutional Aid
- Larger prize amounts

- Renewable
- Must be used at that school
- A student's "numbers" are often most important
- May not require a separate application
- Opportunities for more aid may arise once a student is enrolled
- Limited number of scholarship opportunities at each school
- Deadlines for scholarship consideration
- May require admissions application be filed early (This is not the same as Early Action or Early Decision.)

Private Merit Aid

- Smaller prizes
- Usually not renewable
- Not tied to one college
- Many opportunities to win private merit aid
- Deadlines are year-round
- Not based heavily on GPA or standardized test scores
- Scholarships available for a huge range of types of achievement
- New private scholarships continually emerging

3. **Do we earn too much money to qualify for merit**

scholarships?

No. Merit scholarships are awarded without consideration of financial need. They reward excellence in a given area of achievement. The providing organization strives to help a student pay for college and realize their potential.

I strongly believe that the validation that merit award winners receive can be as valuable as the financial benefits. Students win merit scholarships based on their own efforts. It's also very empowering for students to contribute to the cost of their college education.

Meanwhile, colleges have been known to take away a hybrid or need-based scholarship if a student submits false or incorrect financial information or appears to have been dishonest about reporting their level of financial need. As a reminder, a family's financial situation does not impact the winning of scholarships that are based entirely on merit.

Even if you can pay the whole college bill, why would you want to?!

Even the wealthiest families can win merit aid. There are many reasons a family that can afford to pay for their student's top choice college will pursue merit scholarships. These reasons include the belief in the value of a student contributing to the cost of their college education.

4. How much time do scholarships take?

Consider this: if a student spends even five hours on a merit scholarship application (which would be rare) and wins $500, then they would have earned $100 per hour! If they win $1,000 and spend the same amount of time, that's $200 per hour. Better yet, if they recycle an essay they wrote for another purpose and take two hours to apply for a $1,000 scholarship, then that translates into $500 per hour. That's a lot of hamburgers to flip at a typical high school job!

Although families often ask how long their student will need to spend on scholarships, there are too many variables to answer with much accuracy. Some students write more quickly than others. Furthermore, some scholarships are easier to find and have shorter applications.

On the other hand, the largest private merit scholarships may require extensive research. In this case, the payoff is that a student can receive tens of thousands of dollars of "free" money for college!

Of course, merit scholarships are not really "free" in the sense of not requiring any work. They do indeed require time, effort, and strategy.

The more well-chosen scholarships a student applies for, the more chances to win money for college that doesn't have to be repaid!

The customized lists of merit scholarships I prepare for each of my private clients contain a variety of types of scholarships with a range of deadlines, complexity of the applications, and expected competition levels. Some ask students to create a video rather than write an essay. The variety is endless.

Researching scholarships for ones that fit a particular student is often the most time-consuming part of the scholarship process. The sooner the family begins researching scholarships, the less the chance for missing deadlines and the more opportunities to win money for college that doesn't have to be paid back.

Being organized is vital to saving time, preventing last minute panic, and not missing deadlines. Together, these factors can mean more scholarship winnings.

Tips for saving time and staying organized:

Getting into college is one thing. Paying for it is another.®

Make a scholarship calendar. Inclu when the student will work on applications, edit. Also, mark blocks of time for research an any letters of recommendation that may be requi

Create a new email address for your sch ship research. Use that email when submitting student profiles on the large scholarship database sites. This will keep incoming emails alerting you to new scholarships in one place and help you stay organized.

To save even more time and effort, look for scholarships that provide opportunities to "recycle" essays the student has previously written. There is nothing wrong with students using their own work multiple times. Of course, it's not okay to copy someone else's writing!

5. Are there really merit scholarships for my student even if he/she isn't a great student or the best athlete?

Most likely, yes. I have not met a student yet for whom I could not find at least $25,000 of private merit scholarships they were eligible to receive. (I find as much as $200,000 in private merit scholarships for each of my private clients, and that doesn't include money from colleges!)

There are private merit scholarships for everything from baking the best apple pie, to analyzing a famous literary work, creating a video on drinking responsibly, ebating a political issue, and the list goes on virtually indefinitely!

Generally speaking, grades and standardized test scores matter more for institutional merit scholarships than for private scholarships. Judges for private scholarships want to support students whose achievements, interests, and goals match the group's mission. Many private scholarship providers weigh commitment, leadership skills, and passion more heavily than academic or athletic excellence.

For instance, David Letterman gives $10,000 to a student with average grades who demonstrates exceptional creativity, and the "GPA Isn't Everything Scholarship" rewards aspiring college students who struggle academically in high school.

The trick is finding scholarships that match what makes a student unique, understanding the organization's mission, and presenting the student in the way that most closely supports that mission.

6. How do we find merit scholarships? We don't know where to start.

The sooner you start the process the more scholarships you'll find and the more opportunities you'll have to pay less for college.

There are some scholarships for middle school students; however, the majority are for high school students. The largest number of private scholarships are for graduating seniors.

Begin with local scholarships. High school guidance counselors, local newspapers, neighborhood businesses, and charitable groups are great resources. Spread the word that your student is looking for scholarships! Make it known in your social, religious, and business circles.

Research Tips:

- Keep a scholarship file. Collect flyers, newspaper articles, and website addresses that announce upcoming scholarships. Clip articles announcing local scholarship winners and save the information for next year. Even if your student will no longer qualify, a younger sibling or friend might be eligible.

- Team-up with another family and be on the lookout for scholarships that fit one another.

- Ask your high school guidance counselor about scholarships that neighborhood students have previously won.

- Let large databases such as www.fastweb.com and www.scholarships.com do some of the research for you. Expect to receive many scholarship "matches" that don't fit your student, as well as scholarships that are appropriate. You'll need to carefully read the profile for each scholarship opportunity to be sure your student meets all the requirements. This is the most time-consuming (and frustrating) aspect of scholarship research.

- Use Google and other search engines to uncover scholarships that focus on your student's various achievements and experiences. If your student excels in community service, for instance, type "community service scholarships" and the current year into the search box. Including the year is important so you don't receive information about scholarships that have expired.

- Scholarship reference books quickly become outdated. However, some do offer the benefit of grouping scholarships by state, area of interest, and other categories. This narrows down the search process and can introduce you to new scholarship opportunities to explore.

- The more specific the eligibility requirements for a particular merit scholarship, the smaller the pool of qualified applicants. This means less competition, which is a bonus!

- Think like a detective and follow the trail from one scholarship to another. This can actually be fun...like looking for a buried treasure. Admittedly, you'll hit many dead-ends, but when you find one that works, it feels as though you've struck gold even before winning any money!

7. **Are there merit scholarships for students who are already in college?**

Yes! Most private scholarships are for in-coming college freshmen. However, both private and institutional aid merit aid does indeed exist for upper classmen as well.

These opportunities can be harder to find, but may have less competition because fewer people take the time to look for them.

In addition, colleges may award merit aid to existing students. Financial aid officers and department chairs are great resources for these opportunities. Remind your student to always keep their eyes open for chances to win money for college.

There are merit scholarships specific to all types of students, from mothers returning to college, to veterans who are seeking an education. Merit aid also exists for graduate study, both locally and abroad. It's especially important to read the fine print when researching scholarships for studying abroad, or for citizens of foreign countries who want to study in America.

Again, the good news is that opportunities are out there. The challenge is finding the right scholarships that match your student's circumstances.

8. **Are scholarships really worth the effort if there's no guarantee of winning any money?**

Absolutely!

Without the effort, there is a guarantee that your student won't be awarded private merit scholarships! The more well-chosen scholarships they apply for, the more money they can win.

Many colleges automatically consider all admitted candidates for merit scholarships without a separate application. Oftentimes, the student must submit their application for admission by early fall to be considered for these scholarships. Be sure to read carefully the financial aid and scholarship pages of the websites for the colleges your student is considering.

These sections of college websites may be visited by only 10% of those who view the home page. This means less competition for scholarships announced on those pages!

9. **Local scholarships usually don't offer as much money; should we focus only on national scholarships?**

I recommend a mixture of local and national scholarships. Although the prizes are often smaller, the competition for local scholarships is far less than for nationally publicized ones which can receive more than 100,000 applications per year! Every little bit counts. Smaller scholarships can add up.

Be sure to choose letters of recommendation wisely; it's likely that the local scholarship judges know high school faculty and community leaders who are writing the letters.

Look for announcements about local scholarships in Starbucks, the community newspaper, and posts on library bulletin boards. Ask businesses, religious organizations, and charity group leaders if they know about any merit scholarships being offered.

Getting into college is one thing. Paying for it is another.®

10.   Is it too late to apply for scholarships?

That depends on your goals.

There are always more merit scholarships, even after the student has started college. However, finding a scholarship that perfectly matches your student's achievements after the deadline is heart-breaking! Furthermore, deadlines for many scholarships are in fall or winter of senior year.

The more specific the scholarship requirements, the fewer students are qualified to compete. These are the best one to find! In addition, competition often increases as more students finally realize they need to pursue merit aid and they must scramble to find ways to lower college costs.

However, if your family needs to know how much merit aid the student has available prior to committing to a college, then they need to apply for scholarships that announce winners prior to National Deposit Day on May 1 each year.

Private merit scholarships are available year-round. This means that there are always more scholarships to apply for; however, the vast majority of deadlines are before the spring semester of senior year in high school!

I have had clients come to me at that time and we pursue scholarship money that can be used during the second term, rather than the fall term. Remember that it takes time to receive the money after winners have been determined.

11. How much merit aid are we allowed to receive?

Without getting too specific (and making this confusing), colleges generally place a limit on how much combined need-based and merit aid a student can receive.

Most colleges have strict policies preventing students from receiving more scholarship money than the actual cost of attending that school.

Winning private merit aid can sometimes prompt a college to reduce the amount of need-based aid the student receives. It's best to contact each school directly. Colleges vary greatly on many issues, including scholarships!

Questions You SHOULD Ask!

Families need answers to their questions before they can most successfully tackle the scholarship process and craft a game plan to win money for college. The most frequently asked questions were those we just have covered. Sometimes, however, the questions they DON'T ask are as important, if not more so, than the questions that they do pose.

The following is a list of questions families should be asking about scholarships, but typically don't do so. The list is the result of hundreds of hours of research and my real-life experiences working with a variety of college-bound families who have different goals, challenges, and achievements. These responses contain important information to save you time, reduce stress, and maximize your student's potential. These three ideals are also the basis for my company, Three Wishes Scholarships.

1. **How can my student qualify for more merit scholarships?**

Generally speaking, colleges rely heavily on a student's GPA and standardized test scores to determine who receives institutional merit aid and how much money the student will be offered. Therefore, I recommend students work with an experienced SAT or ACT tutor if possible. Maintaining a high GPA is also important.

Consequently, an academic tutor is often a wise investment because GPA and rigor of coursework are factors in awarding institutional merit scholarships. Certainly, SAT/ACT and academic tutoring also contribute to college admissions success.

In addition, extensive hands-on experience related to the student's college major can indeed lead to generous institutional merit scholarships. This was the case for my youngest daughter, Kayla, who received large scholarships from four high-ranking universities in her field.

Students need to develop a passion for something and a track record of commitment to it. I strongly recommend students engage in well-chosen community service for an extended period of time. This greatly helps in securing private and institutional merit scholarships, as well as with admissions.

To win admission to the most prestigious colleges, a student must be more than their numbers.

This is one arena where GPA and standardized test scores are critical. There are currently only 19,000 freshmen in the Ivies combined. With about 40,000 high schools nationwide and each having at least one valedictorian (our local high school had 26 in 2012), even

Getting into college is one thing. Paying for it is another.®

some valedictorians will not be admitted to an Ivy League school.

Indeed, colleges increasingly reward students who are exceptional in both academic and non-academic ways.

Admissions officers know that all applicants have 24 hours in each day to better themselves and the planet. Colleges evaluate how a high school student spends their time as an indicator of whether that student will make a positive contribution to their college.

Community service is the great equalizer.

All students can excel at giving back and contributing their time, talents, and energy to making the world better in some way. Meanwhile, regardless of how much tutoring they receive, not all students will excel on standardized tests or ace math, science, and English classes.

I have seen repeatedly how community service can offset a lower GPA and SAT/ACT scores, tipping the student into the group of admitted students and scholarship winners.

Many private merit scholarships specifically seek to reward students for community service. In other cases, scholarship essay questions touch upon community service

48

to such an extent that a thoughtful response revolving around the student's demonstrated leadership, commitment, and contribution will satisfy a wide range of scholarship essay questions.

For instance, essay prompts revolving around the following topics are ideally suited to a discussion about one's community service involvement: life lessons, most impactful experiences, role models, acquired skills, future goals, and how the student will contribute to their college community.

Special Bonus from Nancy

Now that you have your copy of *The Little Book About Scholarships*, you are on your way to using your student's achievements to pay less for college! Plus there are tons of other benefits to our kids having "skin in the game" beyond the money.

You'll also receive the special bonus I created to add to your bag of tricks ... *Grade-by-Grade Guide to Pay Less for College*, which is a grade-by-grade checklist of what to do now to save on college later.

There's so much confusing information out there. When you finish this book you'll be armed with what you need to know and answers to the most common questions about merit scholarships to get you up to speed and on the right track fast!

While this Guide is offered for sale, as a special bonus you can claim it for free here:

        http://ThreeWishesScholarships.com/bookbonus/

The sooner you know how merit scholarships can work for your family, the better your chances for cutting college costs.

I'm in your corner. Let me know if I can help further.

Write info@ThreeWishesScholarships.com or call (855) 4-3WISHES.

Here's to paying less for college!

Best,

Getting into college is one thing. Paying for it is another.®

2. When should we start thinking about how to make our student stand out in the college process?

In the eyes of most admissions officers and scholarship judges, a student's high school career begins the day after 8th grade graduation. The summer before high school can be an ideal time to begin sampling a variety of meaningful extra-curricular involvements for a few that the student will ultimately give a lot of time and energy.

3. There are so many merit scholarships, how do we decide which ones to apply for?

The better the student fits the eligibility requirements of a scholarship, the stronger contender he/she will be to win it. Also, the student should learn as much as possible about the providing organization and its mission before starting the application. This information will be very important for weaving the student's achievements into essays and throughout the scholarship application.

Students need to present themselves as the candidate the scholarship judges have been hoping to find.

Getting into college is one thing. Paying for it is another.®

Among the scholarships that the student is eligible to receive, look for a common theme among several of the essay questions. This will save the student time. With some minor edits, they can use the same essay multiple times.

Unless indicated otherwise, it's perfectly acceptable for a student to use their own work in more than one place.

In fact, The Gen and Kelly Tanabe Scholarship strongly encourages applicants to submit existing essays.

The more a student can multi-purpose their essays, the more scholarship applications they will have time to complete. Winning merit scholarships is largely a numbers game; the more one applies for, the more money they can win.

4.   What makes a good scholarship essay?

Scholarship judges want to feel as though they know the winning candidate. Essays that bring about emotion in the reader are often the strongest. It's advisable to paint a picture using descriptive words and images.

Oftentimes, writing about something meaningful that isn't already covered in another section of the application is a good strategy. The student needs to be sure to answer the question being asked; otherwise, it might appear as though the essay was written for another scholarship competition. Again, it's important to demonstrate an understanding of the organization that is sponsoring the scholarship, its mission, and how the student reflects those values.

Following directions is vital, and failure to do so is a common complaint of scholarship judges. You can help your student by reviewing the scholarship application and instructions. Make note of whether the application calls for 250 words or 250 characters, for example. Don't submit transcripts or a letter of recommendation unless instructed.

Meet all deadlines. Online applications may even require that applications be received by a particular time; therefore, pay close attention to whether the deadline refers to Pacific or Eastern Time. Also remember that scholarship websites can become jammed as deadlines approach. A great application that arrives after the deadline won't result in money for college!

Checking for errors is a critical step in the application process. Offer to edit your student's essays and proofread the application. Understand, however, that they may select someone else to do their editing, such as an English teacher.

5. **How can my student increase their chances of receiving institutional merit scholarships?**

Be over-qualified.

Colleges award merit scholarships to students they most want to accept their invitation to attend their school. Generally speaking, students who receive the largest institutional merit scholarships have standardized test scores and GPAs that are higher than the average scores of either: other students applying for admission that year; the average score of students admitted the previous year; or the average of the entire student body at that time.

Unfortunately, there's no exact science to explain how colleges award merit aid or to know with certainty how much aid a student will be offered. Understanding the practices at each school on your student's college list, however, is part of a comprehensive game plan to reduce the cost of college.

Institutional merit aid usually offers the best way to substantially lower the cost of a college education. The amounts of these awards are typically much larger than private merit scholarships. Scholarships from colleges are usually renewable, assuming that the student maintains a minimum GPA, takes the required amount of credits each term, and meets any other requirements that may exist.

My daughters have received institutional merit scholarship offers ranging from $8,000 to $90,000 per school over four years! That's quite a range and a significant reduction in the sticker price!

One benefit of institutional aid being renewable is that the family has an idea of how much a particular college will cost before the student has to officially commit to attending. Meanwhile, the student can continue to pursue private merit aid each year to lower college costs even more. Some colleges now even offer fixed rate tuition; the price that exists when the student enters as a freshman will be the same when they are at the school four years later.

Last fall, I received a call from a frantic grandmother who had recently paid the tuition and housing fees for her granddaughter, a freshman at a large public university. The grandmother was furious at her daughter -- the college student's mother -- for not finding and applying for merit scholarships. Furthermore, the family had chosen that college without a way to pay for it which magnified the problem.

Note: I have my own opinions about whose responsibility it ultimately is to find and apply for merit scholarships and increase one's options about where their family can afford to send them to college. (Can you guess what those opinions might be?)

Getting into college is one thing. Paying for it is another.®

6. **How do we know what price range to look in if we don't know if our student will receive any merit scholarships?**

I highly encourage families to include financially "safe" schools on the student's college list. College counselors advise students to apply to a range of colleges with different degrees of selectivity in terms of admissions. They stress the importance of applying to "safety," "target," and "reach" schools.

My perspective is slightly different. I advise families to include schools with a range of sticker prices -- the cost without any merit aid or other financial assistance.

To meet my definition, financially safe schools are those that the family can most easily afford. They often have less competitive admissions requirements, and the student's GPA and standardized test scores fall well within the boundaries of the averages published by the college. Adding schools that fit these criteria often means opening the student's mind to schools they may not have otherwise considered.

Focused on helping families reduce the cost of college, I strongly believe that the price a family will ultimately pay for a particular school may be the single most important factor in determining where the student ultimately attends.

Getting into college is one thing. Paying for it is another.®

The amount of financial burden that college will put on the family could impact the family long after the fading of memories of the great college town, lively social environment, or winning football team.

7.   When should we start researching scholarships?

The sooner your family begins the better. There are a limited number of scholarships for 9th and 10th graders, and less for middle school students. However, getting your student in the practice of submitting scholarship applications as a freshman sets the stage for what is expected later.

Scholarship research can become more of a priority when the student is a junior. Realistically, most families do not have scholarships on their radar until junior or senior year when they start thinking more seriously about college and how to pay for it. Waiting until senior year of high school to plan for merit scholarships is too late.

Students must build their eligibility so they will qualify for more merit scholarships. Waiting until midway through senior year is too late to receive as much merit aid as possible. Finding a scholarship early gives the student time to increase their eligibility for that scholarship.

One of my clients, for instance, met most of the requirements to be a Disney Scholar. She had 85 hours of

58

community service completed. The award required 100 hours. Because I identified the opportunity while she was a junior, she had plenty of time to gain the additional hours and qualify for that scholarship.

Planning early also reduces last minute panic. Students can more thoughtfully space out the deadlines for their scholarships and even complete some applications early.

Furthermore, some merit scholarship providers run more than one contest per year. This allows students who do not win the first time to re-submit an application with very little additional effort.

Merit scholarships are largely a numbers game. The more well-chosen scholarships a student applies for, the more opportunities to win money for college.

8.   Are there other ways to reduce college costs?

Students who spend their extra-curricular time and energy exploring career interests, can get a big jump on narrowing down college majors, which in turn, reduces college costs by minimizing the likelihood of switching majors. Changing majors can cost the student both time and money.

For five years, my youngest daughter, Kayla, volunteered at a camp for children with special needs. Through this community service experience, she identified her career goals of studying speech and hearing sciences and working with special needs children.

Kayla was offered very generous institutional merit scholarships from the #1 and #6 ranked universities in her field, even though her "numbers" were not as high as those universities typically require for admittance.

In total, Kayla was offered $152,000 in merit scholarships. She was also admitted to 13 of the 14 colleges she applied to. Community service was her winning involvement!

Getting into college is one thing. Paying for it is another.®

9.   How can I help my student win money for college?

Encourage your student to take the scholarship process seriously. After all, there are potentially large amounts of money at stake, which can have a big impact on the entire family. Without scholarships, the student may be saddled with loans or have to go to a less expensive college, rather than one of their top choice schools.

The reality is that no school or private scholarship provider owes your family money. They simply don't. Your student needs to earn it in one way or another.

Cleaning up the beach twice a year simply isn't enough. I understand that your student is busy – they all are. But families, who truly want to pursue merit scholarships and reduce the cost of college, realize that they must actively participate in the process. There are certainly many other reasons to encourage your teen to get involved in community service in addition to enhancing college admissions and merit scholarships.

You can help your student research scholarships. This includes asking your business and social contacts if they know of any merit scholarships that would be appropriate for your family.

Getting into college is one thing. Paying for it is another.®

Let your student know the importance of devoting time and energy to merit scholarships. You can also brainstorm answers to essay questions, offer to edit essays, and remind your student about upcoming scholarship deadlines.

10. Are there other benefits to winning merit scholarships in addition to financial relief?

Most definitely!

The money that scholarships bring is certainly important. However, scholarships offer much more than financial rewards. Helping pay for one's college education brings students a sense of accomplishment and pride.

Awarded for achievement, merit scholarships celebrate a student's excellence in academics, leadership, community service, athletics, writing, and many more areas. Being acknowledged for one's commitment and talents validates their hard work and successes.

Receiving a merit scholarship is an honor and adds another layer of credentials to a student's resume. Some merit scholarships include exclusive networking opportunities, as well as future job advantages because many employers look positively at merit scholarship winners.

Putting forth the effort that merit scholarships require is a valuable exercise in taking control over one's life and pursuing goals.

It gives our children a chance to contribute to the cost of their own education. For some, this is a great way to curb entitlement issues. Also, pursuing scholarships minimizes the guilt other students feel about the financial burden college has on their family.

Indeed, scholarships are about more than money. Here are a few words that come to mind: accomplishment, validation, pride, responsibility, contribution, empowerment, independence, opportunity, and success.

Wrapping It All Up

There is indeed a lot to know about merit scholarships. The more a family understands how scholarships work, where to find them, and how to increase eligibility for more scholarships, the better results they can realistically hope to achieve.

Whatever our financial situation, we as parents often feel pressured to make the wisest choices when it comes to paying for our children's college education. How we decide to handle that expense can have an impact on our family's finances for many years. The money has to come from somewhere, after all!

Will a more expensive school bring advantages that outweigh the impact of cost on our family budget, possibly for decades to come? Should our students contribute to the cost of college, and if so, in what way, and to what degree?

From my own experiences and talking with clients and other parents, it has become increasingly clear to me that pursuing merit scholarships offers so much more than the possibility of relief from the financial burdens of college.

By guiding our students to pursue merit scholarships, we empower them to contribute to the cost of their education and learn priceless life skills.

Getting into college is one thing. Paying for it is another.®

Merit scholarships validate their achievements and bolster their confidence and sense of purpose. Winning money for college demonstrates that they are able to play a role in making their college dreams become reality and take some control over their lives.

My goal was to offer you an overview of scholarships (mostly merit-based), which you could digest in a very short time. However, there are many details about scholarships that are important to know on a case-by-case basis. Financial aid officers can be a wealth of critical information. Private scholarships list contact phone numbers and email addresses on their websites for additional guidance.

Too many families remain overwhelmed and confused about how merit scholarships can help their family. They don't know how their student's interests and achievements can lead to money for college until it is too late.

A plan to use merit scholarships to lower college costs really begins long before the research of scholarships. Oftentimes, college-bound families seek my guidance as they are gearing-up to apply to colleges. Some even wait until after their student has committed to attend (and pay for) a particular school.

Once the student is a high school senior, we can only pursue scholarship opportunities that reward the achievements the student has already mastered. It's too late to increase their eligibility for more merit aid.

A much better plan is to begin thinking about scholarships when the student enters high school. By choosing activities and academics wisely, the family will be setting the stage for greater success with scholarships, college admissions, and more.

I firmly believe that well-chosen community service is the very best investment of time and energy for our teens. As parents, we can model the importance of giving back by volunteering with our children, starting when they are young.

In my family, some of our favorite memories involve volunteering together. Each of my daughters has developed her own passion for community service, which enhances their lives in many ways -- including scholarships.

Let's continue this dialogue. Please accept my invitation to stay connected and learn more about merit scholarships and other ways to enhance your student's college experience.

Be sure to sign up to receive my complimentary newsletter at www.ThreeWishesScholarships.com. Please invite other college-bound families and those who care about them to join us, too.

Wishing your family success with scholarships, college, and life!

Nancy.

About The Author

Nancy Paul founded Three Wishes Scholarships – named after her three daughters – to help families use merit scholarships and community service to address the reality that "Getting into college is one thing. Paying for it is another."®

Nancy helps college-bound families nationwide save time, reduce stress, and maximize their potential to win merit scholarships -- money for college based on achievement.

She consults with families to realize their college dreams without breaking the bank! Nancy believes strongly in the many benefits of pursuing merit scholarships that go beyond the financial component. Her clients appreciate her hands-on consulting style and her commitment to giving students the competitive edge in college and in life.

Nancy finds $25,000-$200,000 in private merit scholarship opportunities for each of her private clients. She also advises families on winning as much as $300,000 in institutional aid per student.

Passionate about the many benefits of community service for teens, Nancy also directs teens to leverage their community service to reduce the cost of college, enhance college admissions, pinpoint career interests, develop a sense of purpose, and experience the joys of giving back.

Getting into college is one thing. Paying for it is another.®

Previously, Nancy managed community service partnerships for ABC-TV's "MacGyver" and other celebrities, working on projects with The White House, The U.S. Olympic Hockey Team, The National PTA, The United States Postal Service, and local charities.

Nancy serves as a scholarship judge for one of the world's highest-ranked universities. She is also a contributor to the Amazon best-seller *1,000 Tips for Teenagers* (December 2012).

She speaks, writes, and consults on a range of topics revolving around how to find and qualify for merit scholarships and the value of community service. She is known for being engaging, knowledgeable, and dedicated.

For more information about working with Nancy, or to have her speak to your group, please contact:

info@ThreeWishesScholarships.com
or call (855-4-3WISHES).

Visit www.ThreeWishesScholarships.com and sign up for her complimentary newsletter to stay informed of the latest scholarship news and advice.

Nancy Paul of Three Wishes Scholarships helps families just like yours...

"Thank you for the great book and information! The points I thought were most important were about beating the deadline, knowing the audience/their rules and that every little bit helps. I used to wait until the day before the deadline to apply. The info on writing essays - it definitely helped!! Also, understanding that every little bit helps is something my mother used to say to me when I would moan and groan over applying to a bunch of scholarships for $500 each. At the time, it seemed pointless, but those quick and small scholarships eventually turn into a large amount of money saved!

Mikayla A., student

"Thank you, Nancy! I'm actually trying to help out my sister. She's completely paying out of pocket so research to find resources for someone like her is appreciated. Thanks so much for *The Little Book About Scholarships*."

Mona

"Thank you very much for the helpful information!"

Julia and Liliana R.

"Your mission holds tremendous value for all families facing the daunting process of helping children become the people they aspire to become. As parents we often spend money on things we think will benefit our children, such as private sports lessons, tutors and an array of club memberships when in fact, it makes more sense to be mindful of investing our time and resources in areas with proven outcome based results. Like your services!

Had all of my offspring met you prior to college, our family would have likely been spared tens of thousands of dollars! Plus the priceless years of costly indecision and the emotional toll of changing course mid-stream many times over! There truly is no specific dollar amount I can attach to the aforementioned. I can, without qualification, attest to the fact that what Three Wishes Scholarships grants in terms of making quality education and solid career choices is invaluable.

You are like the retirement fairy for parents (we don't have to spend it all on the kids' college) and the guidance counselor for children seeking a life filled with purposeful passion. I wholeheartedly agree that community service is the great equalizer and highly recommend families invest in your advice in order to create a winning outcome and fulfilling life for all family members."

Beth P., parent

"Thank you for your wonderful knowledge on college scholarships. You are such a wealth of information and we greatly appreciate you!"

Derrick I., Rotary Club

"Thank you so very much for lighting the way for us!"
Maria Helena S., parent

"Our investment in Three Wishes Scholarships is paying
off in ways I couldn't have imagined. The scholarships Eric
is being awarded are important, for sure, but they actually
pale in comparison to the life lessons he learned through
the relationships he developed with Three Wishes
Scholarships."
Dr. Bob U., parent

"Today you really need help navigating every scholarship
avenue so the cost of college is more affordable. Three
Wishes Scholarships helps you achieve this goal."
Ken and Linda S., parents

"We felt like we had run out of options for our son, who is
a stellar student, but the scholarships were not just pouring
in. Nancy helped us discover that there were so many more
options that we never even considered.

Her vast knowledge of the scholarship subject matter really
encouraged us AND she provided us with an excellent road
map that was custom for my son to utilize in his search for
merit scholarships. Nancy showed us a "different view" of

Getting into college is one thing. Paying for it is another.®

applying for scholarships, and gave us very specific, tailored advice that would allow my son to stand out in the crowd. Thank you so much Nancy, for your help and assistance."

LaShawne H., parent

"I highly recommend Three Wishes Scholarship's services for anyone who is looking for scholarships."

Camille B., student

"I expected to receive a listing of scholarships with a brief summary of each -- but I received so much more!!"

Denise B., parent

"I was surprised at how well you able to match my scholarship opportunities to the qualities you knew about me in order to put together a really well suited report.

It's clear by how quickly you compiled such a detailed scholarship report that you spared no effort and I am so grateful for that.

After looking at the opportunities you gave to me, I feel really confident that I have an excellent chance of success for many of these scholarships."

Eric U., student

Getting into college is one thing. Paying for it is another.®

73

"Three Wishes Scholarships lit our path through the track
of paying for college."
Danielle S., student

The WISHES step-by-step system helps families:

Save time understanding how to use merit scholarships as a solution to helping realize their dreams for a college education;

Reduce stress and enjoy a feeling of relief in leaving the scholarship research to us so they can focus on other aspects of the college process;

Maximize potential for winning money for college that does not need to be repaid with a step-by-step system for finding targeted merit scholarships and increasing a student's eligibility for more scholarships.

Special Bonus from Nancy

Now that you have your copy of *The Little Book About Scholarships*, you are on your way to using your student's achievements to pay less for college! Plus there are tons of other benefits to our kids having "skin in the game" beyond the money.

You'll also receive the special bonus I created to add to your bag of tricks ... *Grade-by-Grade Guide to Pay Less for College*, which is a grade-by-grade checklist of what to do now to save on college later.

There's so much confusing information out there. Now you're armed with what you need to know and answers to the most common questions about merit scholarships to get you up to speed and on the right track fast!

While this Guide is offered for sale, as a special bonus you can claim it for free here:

http://ThreeWishesScholarships.com/bookbonus/

The sooner you know how merit scholarships can work for your family, the better your chances for cutting college costs.

I'm in your corner. Let me know if I can help further.

Write info@ThreeWishesScholarships.com or call (855) 4-3WISHES.

Here's to paying less for college!

Best,

Nancy.

Getting into college is one thing. Paying for it is another.®

Getting into college is one thing. Paying for it is another.®

40443315R00044